Praise for *21 Ways to Manage the Stuff That Sucks Up Your Time*

"I just read Grace Marshall's short yet powerful guide to taking charge of your time. Don't let the length of this book fool you... I've been more productive in one day than I have in months by implementing just *one* of the 21 tips she offers. This is a very timely read for me with a new book (and companion website) AND 52-part video course to be completed within the next few months. Thanks, Grace! I'm on fire!"

—Kim Miller, HowToSellYourVideos.com

"I could not read this book in one sitting. I had to keep putting it down to take notes! *21 Ways to Manage the Stuff That Sucks Up Your Time* gives you an interesting take on time management and organization skills. There is no excuse for not achieving your goals if you follow the brilliant insights Grace Marshall has cleverly detailed in this easy to read, enjoyable book!"

—Debi Williams DDS, author of *The Greatest Leaders Do the Least*

"As with all the 21 Ways books, *21 Ways to Manage the Stuff that Sucks Up Your Time* is a lifesaver to my business and to my sanity. Marshall uses practical ways that anyone can implement, now, to manage their time in this busy, busy world."

—Yolanda M. Johnson-Bryant, LW Media Group and author of the *That Literary Lady Knows* series

"Grace has written the complete guide for today's busy and crazy world where we are short on time and patience. This book will give you the tools and know how to grab your time back and take control of your days again."

—Simon Jordan, international author, speaker and host of Simon Jordan TV and The Simon Jordan Radio Show, www.SimonJordan.com

"We all want progress, but so many times the little stuff (like email) and the big stuff (perfectionism-driven procrastination) derail us. Grace Marshall's tips, strategies and fresh ideas in *21 Ways to Manage the Stuff that Sucks Up Your Time* will help you get back (and stay) on track. Read, implement, and then enjoy the feeling that comes from actually accomplishing what you set out to do."

—Erin K. Casev, Contributing Editor at SUCCESS magazine and
/enture series

"Grace's book is an incredibly valuable resource for any small business owner. If you follow her tips and tools you'll be amazed at how much extra time you have to focus on the stuff that *really* matters."

—Julie Hall, Women Unlimited and LifestyleEntrepreneur.com

"Let's face it—we're all human and many of us fall prey to bouts of unproductive behaviour from time to time, sometimes despite knowing better. In this book you'll be reminded of the top ways to be more productive all gathered together in one place (itself allowing you to be more productive!). I love the useful suggestions at the end of each Way on how and with whom to implement her tips. I even learned some clever ideas I'll be implementing myself (Way 6 comes to mind!). Finally the three-part structure to the book leaves no productivity stone unturned and allows your mind to focus on one area at a time. An excellent and quick read you'll refer to again and again."

—Felicia J. Slattery, M.A., M.Ad.Ed., best-selling author of *21 Ways to Make Money Speaking* and *Kill the Elevator Speech*

"Grace's book is packed full of useful advice, whether you're a productivity ninja or a productivity novice. It's passionate, engaging and thought-provoking—anyone that quotes X-Men and A.A. Milne is all good with me!"

—Graham Allcott, author of *How to be a Productivity Ninja*

"As a busy mum you *don't* have to feel overwhelmed by the juggle! Grace has brought together simple, practical tips and techniques which will reduce your "busyness," maximize your productivity and best of all—increase your enjoyment as you regain control and fulfilment in your life. Her light, chatty, friendly style is a delight—it's like having a friend right beside you, encouraging you onto success!

—Jenny Flintoft, www.jennyflintoft.com

"Grace writes with pith and knowingness. The challenge is for people to put her simple, incredibly effective insights and tips to work deliberately—when they do they'll be self reinforcing as the results will be plain to see. One for all newly self-employed people amongst others."

—Jessica Chivers, author of *Mothers Work! How to Get a Grip on Guilt* and *Make a Smooth Return to Work*

"*21 Ways to Manage the Stuff that Sucks Up Your Time* is a great read for anyone seeking to maximize their work output. I loved Grace's simple yet effective advice and look forward to incorporating these time saving tips into my daily schedule."

—Lotwina Farodoye, award winning business woman and author

"To anyone who is running a business and finds themselves not being as productive as they could be this book is for you. It has some excellent ideas to get you focussed and organized. As someone who is super-organized I found some great new tricks which I can't wait to implement. It definitely got me thinking about how I can be more efficient with my time whilst running a business."

—Naomi Richards, The Kids Coach

"Grace's book brings together 21 useful ways to help you make the most of your time. Different techniques work for different people, work your way through the ideas to find the ones that work for you."

—Erica Douglas, www.aceinspire.com

"As a high energy person and very passionate about what I do, I want to help everyone all of the time, which has had a negative impact on my time, productivity and work/life balance. This book is so spot on, I felt like I was reading about me! The first time I spoke to Grace she instantly had a calming effect on me. I am never disappointed with anything she shares and this extends to her book. Grace has a knack of making it all less overwhelming and more achievable. I loved the 'Power Hour' and gave it a go... WOW, how could I have not done this before, it made such a difference. Before I would feel guilty not being constantly available for everyone, and even more so if I didn't check my emails and social media every five minutes dare I miss a message. However, with Grace's highly invaluable and easy-to-implement guidance, I have already started to put things into practice and noticing the difference. This book will be forever my guide!!"

—Carmen MacDougall, motivational speaker and founder of
The VA Coaching and Training Company www.vact.co.uk

"If you want a book that is packed full of time management gems but without the filler, *21 Ways to Manage the Stuff that Sucks Up Your Time* is for you! Grace Marshall calls herself a disorganized productivity coach and one gets the feeling when reading this book that she really has "been there, done that" and learnt to be more productive the hard way! Grace writes with a light, friendly style which makes this book a breeze to read. There's no waffle—this is truly a book for busy people and Grace gets straight to the point, offering us gem after gem in quick succession. I defy anyone to finish reading *21 Ways to Manage the Stuff that Sucks Up Your Time* (and it won't suck your time to do so!) and not emerge with at least one fantastic time tip that will make them feel more productive."

—Amanda Alexander M.Sc. B.A. (double hons), PCC (ICF)
Founder and Director, www.coachingmums.com

21 Ways to Manage the Stuff that Sucks Up Your Time

21 WAYS

to **manage** the **stuff** that **sucks up** your time

Grace Marshall

Discover! BOOKS™
an Imprint of Imagine! Books™

High Point, North Carolina

21 Ways™ Series, Book 8

Published by Discover! Books™
an Imprint of Imagine! Books™
PO Box 16268, High Point, NC 27261
contact@artsimagine.com

Imagine! Books™ is an enterprise of Imagine! Studios™
Visit us online at www.artsimagine.com

ISBN 13: 978-1-937944-10-0

First Discover! Books™ printing, August 2012

Dedication

For all those who juggle, who refuse to drop what's important to them, who won't settle for "not enough time." You inspire me.

For clients, colleagues, and friends who keep asking me, "How do I do it? How do I fit everything in?" Answering your question has brought me here. Thank you.

For my children, who remind me every day that time is life.

Acknowledgements

Firstly a big thank you to my friends and family, for all your amazing love, support, and cheerleading, without which this book would not be possible.

Special thanks to:

My publisher, Kristen Eckstein, for inviting me to write this book. Thank you for this amazing opportunity.

Mentors and colleagues, who have encouraged and challenged me to dig deep and see the diamond within. Thank you for believing in me and giving me no option but to believe in myself.

Friends who have written books before me, showing me it can be done.

My awesome clients, especially the 40 Days of Baby Steps group, for holding me accountable to write this book in 40 days. Your questions, challenges, and conversation fuel my passion.

My husband Grante, thank you for your solid support and our wonderful family. Your "go-for-it" attitude inspired me from the day we met.

Introduction

We all have plenty to do and limited time in which to do it. We know life is busy. What gets to us most isn't the big stuff—it's the small, bitty things that suck up our time and take over our day. The distractions and interruptions. Things we didn't plan for. Five-minute jobs that stretch into five hours.

This is a book about how to manage those things, so that you can do life and business on purpose rather than by reaction.

The first part of this book gives you tips on how to take control of the little jobs. The second will help you to stay focused and manage distractions. The third tackles the inner things that suck up your time—and boy do they!

My hope is that you'll use these ideas, tips, and principles in all areas of your business and personal life. So that you have more time for what you choose.

Enjoy!

Grace

Part 1

Take Control!
Ways to Manage the Little Jobs

Batch Your Bits

I sit down to write and turn on the computer.

I check my emails first. Someone's mentioned me on Twitter. Reply to that. Wow, that's a fantastic quotation. Share that on my Facebook page. Fantastic, some feedback on my last post. Thank them and answer questions.

Back to writing. Get my notes out.

There's a reminder here to introduce a networking contact to my Web designer. That's easy; they're both on LinkedIn. While I'm there I'll add my new contacts. Five a day. It's all about regular and consistent action, right?

Done. Where was I? Ah yes, writing. But my tea's gone cold. Better make a new one. Tidy kitchen counter while I'm there. There's that receipt I was looking for. File it before I lose it again.

Back to the desk, hot cup of tea in hand. Oh look, an email. Fantastic, I've been waiting for him to get back to me. Now where's that file I need to send him?

Why is it that you have plenty of time in your day, and yet when you sit down to work, you can't seem to get the one thing done that you wanted to, despite setting aside a whole morning—or even a day—to do it?

It's because the little stuff gets in the way. The stuff you know you need to do, that's not quite big enough to schedule in your calendar—the five-minute jobs that take over your day.

Every time we turn our attention from one thing to another, it takes time to refocus. Re-read the last paragraph you've written. Revisit your notes. Get back into the right headspace. This takes time.

Instead, take control of the bitty jobs by grouping similar tasks together, and tackling them in one go. This is known as batching and allows you to work more efficiently, with more focus and mental clarity.

Batching allows you to take control of the bitty jobs and work more efficiently, with more focus and mental clarity.

Batch your email

Think about it, your postman only comes once or twice a day. Would you welcome him delivering every letter individually? Would you check the door if you hadn't heard a knock in the last few minutes?

Instead of reacting to emails as and when they come in, how about deciding on a set time to read and respond to email. Only turn your email on for that time. If you do need your emails open for other work, then turn off the automatic send and receive.

You can even set up an automatic reply in your email to set expectations for your clients and contacts:

Thank you for your email. I read and respond to all emails every afternoon from 3 to 4 p.m. (insert time zone). You'll hear back from me then.

This saves them time, too. They won't need to chase or check if you've got it, and they'll know exactly when to expect your reply.

Batch tasks that use similar technology

If you're adding contacts to LinkedIn, working from a batch of business cards is quicker than doing them one by one. You only have to log in once. You can copy and paste messages and edit to personalize rather than handcraft each one from scratch.

When you don't need to click between different windows or programs, you are less likely to be distracted.

Batch tasks that use similar headspace

I find writing requires a different headspace than filing. One requires creativity, inspiration, and original thought. The other requires more decisiveness, discipline, and repetition—less thinking and more doing.

Once you are in the right headspace, your work flows. Take advantage of that and group tasks together that require a similar mental approach.

Try it with:

✓ Emails

✓ Social media

✓ Phone calls

✓ Website updates

✓ Making videos

✓ Setting up auto responders

✓ Uploading files

✓ Editing

✓ Filing

✓ Regular, repetitive tasks

WAY 2

Use a Timer

Social media can be a great tool for marketing and growing your business, but only if you use it to help you run your business, rather than allowing it to become something that runs your life. The same goes for any job that has a way of taking over.

A timer can help to safeguard your time by putting boundaries around the little jobs that take over. The beauty is in its simplicity.

Use a kitchen timer, your phone, on online timer—anything that alerts you when your time is up. Set how much time you are willing to devote to the task at hand. Set the timer. Dive into the task at hand, and stop when the timer goes off.

Focus your mind

Using a timer sharpens your focus on what's actually important. Instead of browsing aimlessly and getting distracted with "I'll just have a look at this . . ." and wonder later "what have I actually done?" you can get to the point early and stay focused.

Ask yourself: *What's the best use of my time here? What did I actually come to do?* (see Way 8: Give Purpose)

Speed up your work

Parkinson's Law says our work will expand to fill the amount of time we make available.

So if you give yourself half an hour to do something, you'll get it done. If you have four hours to do the same thing, you'll spend four hours perfecting something that would otherwise only take you thirty minutes to do. (See Way 21 for more about perfectionism.)

We also tend to work more quickly when we know we are being timed.

Get over overwhelm and procrastination

Timers are great for tackling overwhelming or unpleasant tasks that you keep putting off.

The fact that the timer is ticking means that it won't last forever, which makes it more bearable. Seeing the end in sight creates motivation and momentum. The more quickly you get on with it, the sooner it's over (see also Way 16).

Set expectations

If you are working from home and have children around, you'll know that every time you stop to say, "In a minute . . ." it will take time to find your train of thought again.

Kids love to know what to expect. Set your working time and give them the timer, with the promise that when it rings, they will have your full attention.

Try it with:

✓ Social media

✓ Research

✓ Filing

✓ De-cluttering

✓ Bookkeeping

✓ Writing

✓ Me time

✓ Housework

✓ Making decisions

✓ Sales calls

Combine it with:

The Power Hour

It's amazing what you can achieve with one hour of complete focus compared with days of distracted, fragmented attention.

1. Define your purpose. Be completely clear what you are going to work on (see Way 8).

2. Set your timer to an hour.

3. Unplug from all other distractions (see Way 10).

4. Spend that hour working solely on the task at hand.

5. At the end of the hour, give yourself permission to stop with a sense of achievement, or choose to continue working if you find you're "in the flow."

The Pomodoro Technique

Similar to the Power Hour, this technique encourages short, sharp bursts of focused action plus breaks to renew concentration and recharge energy levels.

1. Define your task(s) for each 25-minute slot.

2. Set the timer for 25 minutes.

3. Work solely on that task until the timer rings.

4. Take a 5-minute break.

5. Move onto the next 25-minute Pomodoro (named after the tomato-shaped timer).

6. Take a longer break after every four Pomodoros.

Resources in this Way:

 PomodoroTechnique.com

 See "Power Hour" in Chapter 9 of *How to be a Productivity Ninja* by Graham Allcott

Handle It Once

(or as few times as possible)

Have you ever found something looming on your to-do list that you keep coming back to but never finished? Perhaps an article that's not quite right, even after the twelfth edit or a decision that you keep stopping to mull over but never actually make.

The more times you pick something up to deal with it, the more time the overall job takes. But we can't do everything immediately as it arises. That would be chaos.

This is where the two-minute rule comes in handy.

Two minutes or less? Do it now.

This idea comes from David Allen's *Getting Things Done*, which explains that if an item takes longer to store and track than it does to deal with straight away, it is more efficient to deal with it the first time it's in your hands.

This keeps your two-minute tasks from piling up, taking up room in your to-do list or in-tray and cluttering your mind.

Try it with:

✓ Incoming email and mail—where the action or response takes less than two minutes

✓ Simple yes/no decisions

✓ Quick requests, such as a file that you have to send

✓ School permission slips that require a simple signature

✓ Junk mail that can go straight in the trash

✓ Appointments that can go straight in your calendar

How to ensure this works

1. If it's a two-minute job, it has to be *finished* in two minutes. Done and dusted. If it turns out to be a bigger job than you initially thought,

then organize it for later. Don't spend an hour right now doing a two-minute job.

2. Use the two-minute rule in fluid times, when you're processing emails, dealing with incoming mail, in between meetings, etc. Not when you have blocked out a chunk of time to focus. That's why unplugging from incoming messages is so important when you want to focus (see Way 10).

3. Get familiar with two minutes. Set your timer, so you know when your time is up. Get to know exactly how much you can get done in two minutes, and avoid "time creep."

More than two minutes? Organize it.

How often do you put something down, only to keep picking it up, and move it around different piles before it eventually reaches its final destination? How could you shortcut that journey?

Move it as quickly as possible to the place where it needs to be dealt with, for example:

✓ Incoming invoices go in a batch in your accounts folder, so when you turn your attention to your accounts, the invoices are there ready to be processed.

✓ Things that need discussing with your assistant or business partner go in one place.

✓ A reminder to call someone tomorrow goes straight in your calendar.

✓ Action items go on the appropriate to-do list or project plan.

✓ Great ideas go straight in your ideas bucket (see Way 12).

✓ Things to look up later can be collected somewhere for a batch of freethinking exploration time later.

Resources in this Way:

 Getting Things Done by David Allen

Make Habits

Habits are the things we do without thinking.

Have you ever wasted a whole evening watching TV without being relaxed or entertained, simply because it was on? Been busy all day without any sense of achievement? Said "yes" (again) when you really, really wanted to say "no"?

There are plenty of unhelpful time habits. What makes them powerful is that it feels as if they just happen without your thinking about them. Habits are like a well-worn path in your brain, clearly marked and easy to follow—the path of least resistance.

What if you can use that to your advantage? Create habits that are helpful precisely because they slip under the radar of your conscious brain, bypassing things like indecision, uncertainty, over-thinking, fear, and procrastination.

Habit doesn't have to be a dirty word. It can make things easier and free you up to focus.

Building helpful habits

Step 1: Define your purpose (What and Why)

What would you love to be able to put on auto-pilot? What do you need to make happen on a regular basis, without it taking up all your mental space and energy?

Why is that important? What would that give you (see Way 8)?

Step 2: Identify the resistance

What makes it such a difficult job at the moment? Is it so overwhelming that you don't know where to start? Do you resent spending time on it? Is it something that drains your energy? Is there an underlying belief that's holding you back, for example: *I'm not good enough, I can't do this,* or *What if it all goes wrong?*

Step 3: What small step would bypass that resistance?

What would be easy to do on a regular basis, rather than pile up into a monster of a job?

Writing a book might seem a daunting task. Writing 100 words each day seems much more achievable.

Ten minutes of filing is more palatable than several hours.

Putting receipts into a separate envelope each week is much easier to deal with than having to sort through a pile that has built up over several months.

Step 4: Make the commitment

Decide how much time and energy you are willing to devote and how often. Make it an easy investment.

Set accountability to support your commitment. Check in with a trusted friend, colleague, coach, or mentor. Or declare your commitment and progress publicly.

Step 5: Celebrate each success

Set the habit into motion with one baby step at a time. Count each step you take—don't worry about the odd stumble here and there. Focus on progress. Every step you take makes the path smoother, clearer, and more familiar, and that's when the habit forms.

When it becomes so natural that it continues under the radar, you'll be free to focus your direct attention on whatever you choose.

Try it with:

✓ Marketing

✓ Bookkeeping

✓ Filing

✓ Writing

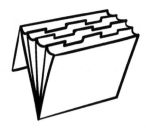

WAY 5

Automate Appointments

It's amazing how much time you can spend to set an appointment with emails going back and forth proposing and counter-proposing dates and times. While you are waiting, something else comes up. Do you hold the slots open, or do you book them in and go back to the first person with revised dates?

Add up the time it takes to think, plan, communicate, negotiate, rethink, replan, and renegotiate. No wonder setting appointments can suck up our time, sometimes more time than the actual appointment itself!

There are several ways to cut this wasted time:

Option 1: Get calendars together and talk

Rather than playing email ping-pong, get together on the phone or face-to-face when you both have your calendars and set an appointment there and then.

Option 2: Have set times for set appointments

One of the senior partners at my local doctor's office only has appointments on Tuesdays between 4 and 6 p.m. Seems a bit restrictive, but this gives her time to tend to her other duties. Similarly, a coach I know has set open office hours when you can call for help.

Having time set aside for particular types of appointments helps to reduce your decision-making time. Offering limited choices also makes it easier for the other person to decide.

Option 3: Automate appointments

This is my favorite option. Use an online appointment system like TimeTrade to automate your booking process. You can define your available times, appointment length, how far in advance people can book, and automatically sync it with your personal calendar to match and update your availability.

I use this for coaching sessions and initial consultations. I simply give my clients the link. They view my available time, compare it with their calendars, make their decisions in their own time and book a slot that suits them.

You can take the automation a step further and link it in with your payment processor or email auto responder, so that once a client has made a payment, he or she automatically gets an email with the link to book the appointment.

Try it with:

✓ Client appointments

✓ Consultations

✓ Meetings

✓ Suppliers

✓ Colleagues

✓ Support Help Desks

Resources in this Way:

 TimeTrade.com

 Aweber Email Auto Responder

Post Networking Post-Its

Networking is a fantastic way to promote and grow your business, but the biggest value comes from following up with the connections you make after the meeting.

This can take time. Considering you've probably just spent the best part of a morning or afternoon getting to and attending the networking event itself, you could easily spend the rest of the day following up with each of them.

What's more likely is that you add the business cards you've collected to the growing pile you already have, and dread the day when you actually decide to go through them. The result? You don't follow up. Or you spend ages looking at each card, trying to figure out where you met them, whether they would be good to connect with again, and how to start that conversation. Either way, it's time-consuming.

Here's what I like to do:

Decide how you will follow up at the meeting

What challenges or topics are they talking about? What would be a useful resource for them: an article, blog post, or information about one of your products? What event or workshop could you invite them to?

Who would be a useful contact for them? Perhaps a potential client, supplier, or collaboration partner.

Decide your follow-up strategy there and then.

Write it on a post-it note and stick it on their business card

When you follow up you can mention the conversation you had and say, "I thought of this when you spoke about that. Hope it's helpful."

I like to take it a step further and actually say how I intend to follow up. I ask if they would like an introduction to that particular contact. I offer to send them the link. I ask if it would be helpful to them if I add them to my newsletter list.

This means when I follow up, I am delivering a promise instead of testing a lead. I don't waste time wondering if it's OK for me to send them something, how to phrase it, or whether it would be considered too pushy. Instead, I have already asked them and they said "yes," which means I can follow up with confidence and say, "as promised, here is. . ."

With clear instructions on those post-it notes, following up becomes a simple task of following through, which bypasses indecision and the procrastination of wondering how and when to follow up.

For another detailed follow-up system, check out Way 18: Follow Up in the book *21 Ways to Powerfully Network Your Business* (Book 2 in this series) by Kristen Eckstein.

Resources in this Way:

 What's the point of networking? Grace-Marshall.com/ whats-the-point-of-networking

 21 Ways to Powerfully Network Your Business by Kristen Eckstein

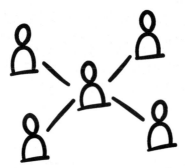

WAY 7

Firefight Like the Pros

Fire-fighting is a word we often use in our work and personal lives to describe the kind of panic and rush that comes with reacting to a crisis, usually as a result of leaving certain things unattended.

Being able to respond to a sudden crisis or opportunity is a good thing, but if you are constantly reacting, you'll find it draining, ineffective, and time-consuming.

Interestingly, that's not how real fire fighters act. Professional fire fighters respond to crises with well-thought-out strategies. Here are three strategies to fight your own fires:

Plan your response

Fire fighters may not be able to predict when there will be an emergency, and their job is certainly not to plan them. However, they have plans and procedures to put into action in an emergency, rather than just purely reacting.

What about your business? What do you find yourself reacting or responding to on a regular basis? What emergencies keep occurring? Do you have a plan or procedure, or do you have to think it through every single time it happens?

Putting a system in place means you can think it through beforehand, decide how best to respond, and then implement it when needed—and more quickly.

This frees up your mind to adapt to unique situations rather than rethinking the same procedures time and time again. It means you act to consistent standards. It becomes easier to delegate or automate, which makes your business more scalable.

Preempt questions

If you spend a lot of your time answering the same kinds of questions, put together a collection of Frequently Asked Questions. Make this available to your customers on your website, so they can access it quickly and conveniently without having to wait for your personal response. Mention it on your voicemail, email acknowledgements, or order receipts. This will save you time and drive traffic to your website.

Set expectations

Cut down on "just checking when . . ." and "what happens next?" questions from your customers by setting the expectations from the outset:

You'll get a confirmation email within the next two hours.

Your item will be arrive by . . .

I'll give you a call tomorrow to discuss . . .

Your proofs will be ready in two weeks.

Tell your customers what to expect, and you will save their time and yours. Give them great service when you deliver on your promises.

Try this with

- ✓ Customer enquiries

- ✓ Sales process

- ✓ Press enquiries

- ✓ Customer service issues

- ✓ Risk assessments

Part 2

Stay Focused!
Ways to Manage Distractions

Give Purpose

"Productivity is never an accident. It is always the result of a commitment to excellence, intelligent planning, and focused effort." —Paul J. Meyer

Purpose is what makes the difference between busyness and business, between activity and productivity.

Without purpose, you can spend hours on Facebook or Twitter with no tangible impact on your business. You can have 500+ connections on LinkedIn without having a single conversation. You can invest time and money into advertising or networking without generating a single lead or sale.

Purpose helps you define your priorities

When everything is equally important, you get overwhelmed with too much to do, too much choice, and too much information. When you know what you want to achieve, you can focus on the activities that make the biggest impact and clearly evaluate between an opportunity and a distraction. Defining your purpose means you will spend less time reacting, chasing tangents, or backtracking.

Purpose gives more focus and less distraction

When I watch my son at swimming lessons, I notice that when he watches other people around him, he starts following them and swims in a zig-zag pattern. When his focus is solely on his own race, he swims in a straight line.

Knowing your purpose means you can fix your focus on what *you* are doing, and avoid the diversion of looking at what other people are doing. You are less likely to go around in circles or end up at someone else's destination rather than your own.

Purpose means you make decisions more quickly

When you know your priorities and have your focus, you spend more time *doing* than *wondering* what to do.

Questions to clarify your purpose

1. **What's the point?** What is the ultimate purpose of what you are trying to achieve with your business—personally and professionally?

2. **What's my primary focus right now** in relation to that purpose? Is it generating leads, building up cash, growing your credibility, or creating products?

3. **How will this best serve that purpose and focus?** How do I use this particular tool, tactic, or task to move forward toward my goal? What will make the biggest difference?

If your primary focus is to promote your book, you can focus your Twitter activity on connecting with the media and key people of influence in your industry, giving tips and quotations, and directing people to download a sample chapter, rather than generally directing people to your website.

Instead of doing everything, do what matters most. Instead of flitting from one thing to another within your business, align all your activity toward a common purpose, and you'll find you achieve better results in less time.

Focus with a Closed List

I love lists. I love being able to write things down, get ideas out of my head, know what I have to do, and get it done. But sometimes you can spend more time making lists, staring at them, and getting demotivated, than actually getting the job done.

Lists work when they help you focus. They stop working when they leave you frustrated.

Keep brain dumps and to-do lists separate

A brain dump is about collecting your thoughts onto paper. It can be a list of all the things you need to do, a collection of ideas, or a mixture of the two. It tends to be free flowing with no real structure. The purpose of a brain dump is to clear your head (see Way 13).

A to-do list is about taking all the possibilities of what you could do, want to do, and have to do, and distilling that into a list of what you *will* do. It is about commitment. The purpose of a to-do list is to enable action.

When you treat your brain dump as a to-do list, there is too much choice, too much to do, and no prioritization. You waste time getting overwhelmed and trying to decide what to do first. You might spend time chasing little jobs rather than working on what actually matters.

Most of all, when your list keeps growing, you lose that sense of progress and completion. Instead of celebrating each job you tick off, you feel more demotivated by the growing size of what's yet to be done. The list becomes a burden and you lose momentum and motivation.

Close that list

An open list grows. If you want to enable completion, then close that list. Instead of working from a brain dump of a hundred different tasks, thoughts, and ideas, create a separate to-do list with a set number of tasks to complete. Be selective.

Once you've decided on your actions, close the list. Draw a line under it and refuse to add any other items. If anything else pops up, add that to your brain dump, or write it under the line. Focus on the tasks above the line. Once those tasks are done, consider your to-do list completed and celebrate that fact! Any extra work you do is a bonus, not a requirement. Any extra time you have is yours to do with as you please.

WAY 10

Unplug without Divorcing

Distractions happen to all of us. You start the day with a list of things to focus on. Then the phone rings, an email comes up, an idea pops into your head, something catches your eye on Facebook— you click a link and end up blog surfing for an hour.

Whatever your distraction, it throws you off course, disrupts your focus, and sucks up your time.

It may feel as if you are busy staying on top of work when you are always on, accessible everywhere, and able to answer messages straight away. The truth is when you're working by reaction, your distractions are controlling you.

When you need to focus, one of the most productive things you can do is unplug.

Unplug

Turn off your emails, Facebook, Twitter, YouTube, and any other social media site. If you need to access your emails for a particular job, turn off the automatic send/receive function so new incoming emails don't distract you.

Close any browser windows that you don't need to use for the task at hand. The fewer things there are to click on, the more you can stay focused.

Divert your phone to voicemail. If you're worried about missing customer calls, make your voicemail message more engaging, humorous, or informative. Turn it into a marketing tool—something you want people to hear. Or use an answering service.

If you work from home, unplug from your household chores by having a designated workspace, or physically move your laundry, ironing pile, personal paperwork, etc. into another room and shut the door.

When working in the evening, communicate to your family when you want to focus. Ask and negotiate for uninterrupted time. Talk about how you can practically put this in place.

Unplug, not divorce

The biggest fear we have of unplugging is that we will unplug for too long or cut off connection completely. We worry we will miss out on opportunities, let down a client, offend an important supplier, or put off an influential journalist. We are afraid of damaging relationships with business contacts, friends, and family.

Divorce is final. Unplugging is temporary, so set your timer for a block of time to focus, or a specific time when you plug into emails, phone, and social media. Then you will know when you will be back in touch and you can communicate that to others to set their expectations.

Unplug from your business

Equally, it is worth unplugging from your business to fully focus on and enjoy your family and home time.

This is so much easier when you have a sense of completion, so plan your work with completion points in mind. Rather than "build website," which could take weeks, break your projects into individual action points—what I call baby steps.

Specify which steps and actions you will get done each day. I suggest a maximum of three to five. Make them your absolute must-dos. Once they are done, consider your day's work complete (see also Way 9).

Enjoy that sense of completion and achievement. Give yourself full permission to stop and switch off so you can rest, recharge, and reward, ready to take on the next day and its steps.

Try it with

✓ Batching (Way 1)

✓ Power Hour (Way 2)

Resources in this Way:

 Answering service:
Answer.co.uk

AnswerConnect
(BBB accredited)

 Specialty Answering Service
(BBB accredited)

 The Power of Baby Steps

WAY 11

Say "No" and Stay Nice

Even when you have your own focus nailed down, distractions and interruptions can come from other people. People who catch you in the middle of something interrupt your flow of thought, and divert your attention onto their focus.

It's frustrating when it feels beyond our control, especially when we find it hard to say, "No." When we stop to respond, we make other people's urgency our priority.

"The most powerful thing you can do in a situation where you have little or no control is to create choices."
—Carrie Wilkerson, *The Barefoot Executive*

You may not have control over what somebody else does, but you do have a choice in how you respond, negotiate, set expectations, and enforce your boundaries.

Say "yes" on your own terms

Saying "no" can feel uncomfortable. If you are worried about appearing rude or uncaring, you'll find it much easier to say "yes" on your own terms.

Instead of, "No, I'm busy" tell them what you *can* do for them. Give alternatives that you are happy with:

I'd love to hear about that. Can we talk at 4?

Absolutely, let's set up a meeting.

I'm available tomorrow at 10 and at 3—which would you prefer?

I can give you a call tomorrow. What times should I avoid? *

* This gives you more flexibility than asking them for a good time.

Give a reason

Give them a reason as to why it's in their best interest that you contact them later. Keep it straightforward and make it attractive for them to do things your way.

I'm just about to jump on a call / I have an appointment / I'm fully committed right now and I want to be able to give you my full and undivided attention, so this is what I propose...

Apply the two-minute rule

Instead of allowing someone's "have you got a minute?" urgency to become your priority for the next hour or more, here's how you can say "yes" with boundaries:

I've got two minutes. What can I do for you?

This gives them the choice of either getting straight to the point, or arranging a more suitable time to talk. You can be even more specific with:

I've got two minutes right now, or we can talk at 4 p.m. Which would be best for you?

Use 'and' rather than 'but'

Instead of: *I want to help you, **but** I'm busy*

Say: *I'd love to help you **and** I can do so at ___*

Say it like it's a good thing

Don't automatically apologize.

Instead of: *I'm sorry; I'm fully booked up for March.*

Say: *I'm now taking client bookings for April.*

As well as being more positive and welcoming to new clients, this suggests your services are in demand.

Say "thank you"

My favorite advice for saying no to cold callers is to thank them. For example, "I'm not looking for ___ but thanks so much for thinking of me."

Many sales callers find this a welcome contrast to the abrupt refusals or vague responses they often get, and are happy to end the conversation on that note. The same goes for invitations to meet with friends or get involved with a project—you can thank them for thinking of you while saying "no."

Practice

Saying "no" is like using a muscle. It gets easier the more you do it (and the more you realize the world really doesn't end when you say it). Take one of these techniques and give it a try this week. Find as many opportunities to practice as you can.

Keep a Tangent Log

Sometimes our biggest distractions do not come from our external environment, but from inside our heads, when our brains come alive with ideas, thoughts, and reminders that have nothing to do with the task at hand.

This is commonly known as the "shiny object syndrome."

My brain is extremely creative when I am trying to focus. Some of my best ideas come when I am concentrating on something else!

However, if I choose to abandon what I am doing and follow that idea, something else will come along and divert me onto another path, and then another, resulting in many great ideas half-started, hours whittled away down rabbit holes, and nothing actually completed, accomplished, or produced.

Capture ideas with a tangent log

One way to capture these brilliant ideas without chasing shiny objects is to keep a tangent log. Keep a notebook next to you when you are focusing. Use it to write down anything that comes to mind that's not relevant to your current focus.

Every time you go off on a tangent, write it down. Capture the thought and get it out of your head, so you don't have to keep remembering it.

Later when the task at hand is done, you can come back to your tangent log, take your pick of which brilliant idea you want to work on next, and work on it purposefully and to completion.

Ideas bucket

Instead of keeping your ideas in a notebook, another variation is to write it down on a sheet of paper (or tear it out of the book) and throw it in a designated bin, bucket, or box. The act of "throwing it away" helps you to remove it from your current focus—out of sight, out of mind. When you are ready to rifle through your ideas, you'll have a bucketful to choose from.

Ideas vs. reminders

You may want to keep a separate log or place for reminders of things you need to get done soon, rather than the ideas that will be nice to explore later.

WAY 13

Empty Your Head

"If you're using half your concentration to look normal, then you're only half paying attention to whatever else you're doing." —Magneto talking to Mystique the shape shifter in *X-Men: First Class*

If we are using our heads to hold things—reminders, pending items, work in progress, things we've yet to make a decision on—we only have part of our mental capacity free to concentrate on whatever we're actually doing.

Write it down to remember

In the early days of motherhood, constantly responding on-demand to my baby, I simply had no capacity in my brain to remember things. This syndrome is otherwise known as "baby brain."

Out of sheer frustration, I started carrying around a tiny notepad and pen in my back pocket. I wrote down every single reminder that popped into my head. Things I needed to do, buy, make, send, look up, discuss, ask, etc. Each item went on a separate sheet. Each day I tore these sheets out and grouped them into batches (see Way 1). Calls to make, errands to run, items to discuss with my husband, and things to do while the baby slept.

I discovered I didn't have to remember. When I had the opportunity to make calls, I had a batch of notes to refer to and work through quickly. This system was far better than stalling at the first hurdle, trying to remember, or kicking myself at 3 a.m. when I eventually did remember.

Write it down to free your mind

Get your reminders out of your head and onto paper to free up thinking space. Concentrate fully on solving that business problem, without the niggling thought that you've run out of milk (unless that *is* your business problem). Focus fully on your children without being distracted by your mental to-do list for the next day.

Write it down to switch off

Your brain is capable of storing a vast amount of information, but it's also made to use that information to think and create. If you are finding it hard to switch off, it may be that your brain is still processing the thoughts that you are holding in your head. When you write things down, you can mentally let go. You are safe to switch off, come back later, and pick up where you left off.

Tools

✓ **Calendar/diary**: Put time-related reminders in your diary or calendar, including relevant information you already have on hand—contact number, location, directions, what to bring, etc. This saves you from having to look it up again nearer the time.

✓ **The humble list**: a to-do list, an ideas list, or a brain dump (see Ways 9 and 12)

✓ **Post-it notes**: Like my pocket notebook, post-its are portable. Write things down on the go. Stick them where you need to remember them—your diary, notebook, the door, or you can stick them together in batches.

✓ **Mind-map**: This is a great way to capture thoughts in a creative way. Use it to brainstorm ideas, organize your tasks, and put together a non-linear visual project plan where you can easily see all the strands that come together to form the whole project.

Because it's non-linear, it highlights flexibility. When things don't go to plan, or simply when you want more variety, you can jump from one strand to another and still make progress toward one common goal.

✓ **Workflowy**: If you prefer to work with linear lists, Workflowy.com is beautifully simple. You can use it to brain dump your thoughts and easily organize all your projects into different groups and categories, zoom in on the detail, and zoom back out to see the bigger picture.

Resources in this Way:

 Mind Mapping:
ThinkBuzan.com

 Free mind-mapping tool:
Freemind.Sourceforge.net

 Workflowy: Workflowy.com

WAY 14

Create Margin

It's tempting to think that productivity is all about squeezing as much as you possibly can into your available time. Not necessarily.

Doing fifty things is not always better than doing five. Busy is neither good nor bad. What matters is *what* we do, not *how much* we do. There's always more to do, but we only feel achievement when we've spent our time doing something we consider to be valuable and meaningful.

In fact, a tightly packed schedule can be counterproductive. It leaves no room for flexibility, adaptability, or creativity. Instead, create margin for free flow—space between your load and your limits, between your capacity and your commitments.

Margin gives you time

Create time to deal with work that overspills, unexpected glitches, and emergencies. It means you can adapt to changes without losing momentum.

Margin gives you flexibility

You have space to change your mind, time to think, and the capacity to respond to the opportunities you could never have planned for. You also have the choice to stop and be pleasantly interrupted by a cuddle, to play, and enjoy the fruits of your labor.

Margin gives you freedom to be creative

You can't always predict when inspiration will strike. While I wouldn't recommend chasing after every idea that comes up (see Way 12), you do want to give yourself time to engage your muse.

Ways to create margin:

✓ Set deadlines and expectations with extra room to maneuver.

✓ Commit to doing five things a day instead of fifty.

✓ Say, "no" to many good things so that you can say "yes" to the best things (see Way 11).

✓ Let someone else do what they can do, so you can do what only you can do

Focus vs. free-flow

Do you prefer to work with structure and focus or a fluid, free-flowing environment?

My most productive days are when I make time for both. Some of my most creative moments and inspired ideas come from free flow, but I need to focus in order to implement and work them through to completion.

Focus and free flow go hand in hand. The value of focus is to bring your free-flow ideas to fruition. Without focus, your free flow has no value. Without free flow, you have nothing to focus on.

One enables the other. They are partners rather than competitors.

Take this analogy: A river has banks to provide structure. This enables the water to flow freely. Without banks, it would be a stagnant pool, rather than a free-flowing river.

Try structuring your day to give you a rhythm of: free flow, focus, free flow. Commit to periods of focus to make sure things get done and delivered, and give yourself space and freedom in between to be creative.

Part 3

Mindset
Ways to Manage the Inner Stuff

WAY 15

Rewrite Worry

Worry takes time and clouds your focus. It prevents you from taking action and making progress, drains your energy, and keeps you from sleeping. It attacks your confidence and steals your peace of mind.

"Worrying is like a rocking chair, it gives you something to do, but it gets you nowhere." —Glenn Turner

Play the "what if" game

"What-iffing" is a skill many of us hone when we worry. We think, *What if it goes wrong? What if I fail? What if everybody hates it?* We imagine the worst-case scenario or a sequence of disasters: *What if that goes wrong ... and that ... and then ...* Which breeds more worry.

"Worrying is using your imagination to create something you don't want." —Abraham Hicks

What if we used our imagination to create what we do want instead? The same skill can be used to build faith when we play the "what if" game in a helpful way:

Step 1 - Flip the question

What if it goes well? What if it goes better than I imagine?

What if I am good enough? What if it's easier than I think?

Step 2 - Take it a step further

What would that mean? What would that give me?

What would the effects be?

Step 3 - Add evidence

When we worry, we come up with all sorts of reasons to back up our disaster thinking.

*Nobody's going to buy **because** it's a recession and nobody's spending any money.*

Equally, you can find evidence to support your positive "what if" statements:

What if people do buy . . .

- ✓ Because people are still spending money

- ✓ Because they love the value we provide

- ✓ Because it's a great product and solves a very real problem for them

- ✓ Because I have taken the time to get to know my customers

Use your imagination. Brainstorm all the possible reasons and evidence you can think of to support your helpful "what ifs."

Step 4 - Turn what if into what is

Highlight the statement that is most powerful for you. Remove the "what if" to rephrase your statement. For example:

I am good enough because . . .

People will buy because . . .

Use these statements to build faith and motivation, and to take the action you need to take to make this true.

Action or Accept

Some things we can't control. Worrying about them won't make any difference, but knowing that isn't always enough. We need something else to focus on instead.

As the serenity prayer goes:

> *Grant me the serenity*
> *to accept the things I cannot change,*
> *Courage to change the things I can,*
> *And wisdom to know the difference.*

An exercise I like to use is Steven Covey's Circles of Influence and Concern:

Step 1

Draw two circles, one inside the other.

Step 2

In the outer circle write all the things you are worrying about—thoughts that take up your time, energy, and headspace. This is your Circle of Concern.

Step 3

In the inner circle, write the things you can actually do something about—actions you can take, resources you can access, people you can ask for help, and things you can do to make a difference. This is your Circle of Influence.

Step 4

Now you can choose to accept the things you cannot change, and direct your energy and attention toward the areas you *can* influence and the actions you *can* take.

Resources in this Way:

 7 Habits of Highly Effective People by Stephen Covey

 More about *What-Iffing: Beliefs and How to Change Them For Good* by Tony Burgess and Julie French

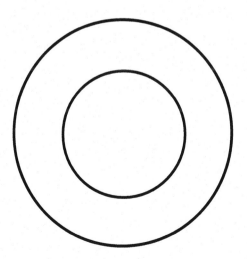

WAY 16

Beat Procrastination

Procrastination has the same effect as worry. You can find a lot of creative ways to occupy your time and mind in order to delay or avoid doing something, which sucks up both your time and your confidence.

Increase desire

One way to overcome procrastination is to make the job more desirable. Desire comes from passion, purpose, and enjoyment. Do what you love and are passionate about, and motivation comes naturally. Even if the task itself doesn't appeal to you, align it with a purpose that you are passionate about. You'll be more motivated and may even find that you enjoy getting it done.

Just as we often turn things into a game, race, or competition to encourage our children to do a task, make it fun for you. Get creative. How can you do it differently to make it more fun?

Reduce resistance

Break it down into baby steps. If something's too big and daunting, break it down into bite-sized, doable chunks to overcome that overwhelming feeling.

Every mammoth project is made up of tiny little steps in the right direction. Define what those steps would be for you and identify the very first step. It might be something as small as getting the file out.

Focus on action rather than worry about results. If the fear of failure (or success) has you avoiding the task, then take the pressure off by focusing on just getting it done.

> *"Failure means I'll do better next time. Inaction means there is no next time."*
> —Michael Masterson, *The Pledge*

Use a timer (see Way 2). Add a reward. The promise of chocolate ice cream can get children to eat their broccoli. What could you bribe yourself with, to sweeten the deal and get it done?

Eat a frog for breakfast

When you pick off the easy and quick wins on your to-do list first, you might find there's one big hairy job that nags at you all day, draining your energy and potentially looming onto the next day if you run out of time.

Eat a frog for breakfast means you take that thing you dread and tackle it *first*. Get it out of the way. Not only will the rest of the day be much easier, you'll feel so good about yourself and what you've achieved, you'll fly through the rest of the day supercharged with confidence. Try it!

JFDI

You can wait, reason, research, analyze, and strategize all you like, but at the end of the day, the only way to get rid of procrastination is to JFDI— Just Flipping Do It. Stop waiting for everything to be perfect (it won't be), or when you're absolutely sure you won't get anything wrong (you will), or when you feel confident enough (that comes *after*). Take a step. Make something happen. JFDI.

See also

Ways 2, 4, 6, 17 and 18

17

Get a Grip on Guilt

When you have multiple roles, such as juggling business and family, you can easily find yourself feeling guilty. You may feel guilty that you should be with your kids when you are working or guilty that you should be working on your business when you are with your kids. Focus on one thing and you'll neglect something else. Time spent in one area is time taken away from another.

This feeling of guilt—being torn between multiple commitments—can drain you of your time, motivation, and energy. As time is already precious, you could probably do without guilt sucking it up. Guilt only ever serves you if it helps to put a finger on something that doesn't feel quite right, like something out of kilter with your values and beliefs. Or something specific you want to change or do differently.

Guilt that generally makes you feel bad as a person is destructive, unproductive, and downright unhelpful. That kind of guilt causes worry, procrastination, indecision, and delay.

Here are the steps to get a grip on guilt:

Step 1 - Check your guilt

What's behind this feeling? What thoughts, beliefs, worries, or fears are causing you to feel guilty?

Step 2 - Challenge your beliefs

Ask yourself, "How true is that, really?" Some underlying beliefs are based on past truths that may no longer reflect today's reality, and some are part truths.

Step 3 - What are the positives?

Often when we are responding to guilt, we only notice what's going wrong. Take some time to acknowledge what is working well and going right, and the potential positives that can come from this situation.

Step 4 - Identify what's important

Rather than focusing on the fear or worry itself, what is it that you value that feels threatened here? Get to the core of what's important.

Step 5 - Clarify positive action

What can you do to honor what's important?

Here are some examples:

Feeling: *I feel guilty that I'm neglecting my children.*

Belief: *If I don't spend enough time with my children they will suffer.*

Challenge it: *What do you mean by enough time? How much time are you spending with them? How are they suffering? Are they suffering? Well, Anna doesn't seem to be happy at school lately. And Charlie says we never get to read anymore.*

Positives: *I do get to pick them up from school now that I run my own business. We didn't have that time before.*

What's important: *My children—their well being and welfare and spending time with them.*

Positive action: *Plan time with children. Be purposeful about when, how often, and what we do (e.g., read with Charlie). Walk home with Anna on Wednesday while Charlie's at football so we can talk about school.*

Feeling: *I feel guilty if I don't respond to clients' emails straight away.*

Belief: *Emails should be answered immediately.*

Challenge it: *Who says? Hmm, me probably. Or maybe that one cranky client years ago.*

Positives: *I have better insights and come up with better solutions when I have time to think. Some of my best responses have been 48-hour turn-arounds, and those clients were very happy.*

What's important: *Reliability and service. I pride myself on delivering on my promises and giving good service, which means I need to respond in a timely manner.*

Positive action: *Set clear expectations of 48-hour turn-around on emails and communicate this to clients. Emphasize quality and meet those expectations every time.*

WAY 18

Build Confidence

Doubt sucks up time in many ways.

We worry about failure and criticism and what people think. We question our own judgment, which can lead to indecisiveness. We question our capabilities, if we have what it takes, and if we can do it at all. All of these doubts can lead to procrastination. (see Ways 15, 16, and 19)

When we are not feeling confident, our focus tends to be driven by the thought, "What will people think?" rather than what gets the job done.

We spend time doing more research to get reassurance, rather than taking the actions that get results. We constantly ask others, "What do you think?" while putting off making our own decisions. We are daunted and distracted by our competition instead of swimming our own race.

Here are three ways to boost your confidence:

Challenge your beliefs

Feelings come from our thoughts and beliefs. If you are feeling under-confident, what thoughts are supporting that?

Are you "disaster" thinking, noting all the things that could go wrong? Are you focusing on your weaknesses, compiling a list of, "Things I'm Rubbish At?" Are you then setting standards of perfection for yourself (see Way 21) and putting your competitors on a pedestal?

"One reason we struggle with insecurity is because we compare our behind-the-scenes with other people's highlight reel." —Steven Furtick

Some of these thoughts may be "true," and some highly exaggerated. Either way, they are not particularly helpful. So what would be more helpful?

Look for evidence

Gather evidence of your strengths, talents, and gifts.

Compile a list of "Things I Am Great At." Note what people repeatedly compliment you on and what they keep asking you for help with. Look at testimonials and case studies of people you have already helped. Make a list of your proudest achievements. Acknowledge what you really enjoyed about it, and what qualities you needed to achieve it.

Build your confidence by focusing on what you're good at, what you can do, what resources you have within you and within reach, and what you've already done.

Get feedback rather than opinion

Whose opinion do you really need to know and understand in order to succeed?

Does it really matter what your mother-in-law thinks about how you run your business? Or does it matter more what your customers and your ideal clients think?

Does it matter what your neighbor thinks about how you raise your children? Or is it more crucial to listen to your family and tailor the way you parent to the needs of your children?

Instead of taking on everybody's opinion, even if they are well meaning and well intentioned, tune into the voices of those who really matter—those who affect and are impacted by your results. Get feedback rather than just mere opinion.

Turn the question around

Instead of self-defeating questions that paralyze you with self-doubt, ask yourself constructive questions.

Is this good enough? **becomes** *What is good about this? What can I improve?*

Am I good enough? **becomes** *What am I great at? How can I use my gifts more?*

I can't. **becomes** *What can I do?* or *How can I?*

WAY 19

Make Decisions!

Indecision can be a real time-sucker. It can stop you from getting started in the first place. Ever sat down to do something and spent the first hour wondering what to do? It can stall you as you try to take action if you question yourself every step of the way.

If your mind isn't made up, chances are you'll keep changing it. You'll go around in circles or take one step forward and two steps back. You'll probably get easily distracted and deterred by doubt (see Way 18).

An unmade decision will keep calling you back to revisit it, taking up valuable time and mental capacity each time. Here are three steps to help you be more decisive:

Step 1 - Separate thinking and doing time

Thinking and doing require different states of mind. One is about processing information, reviewing options, and exploring possibilities. The other is about focused action and unwavering execution.

When we mix the two up, we end up with poorly defined plans and confused action. We spend our time backtracking, stop-starting, and chasing our tails. It's like driving with a misted windscreen and the handbrake on.

"Organizing is what you do before you do something, so that when you do it, it is not all mixed up."
—A.A. Milne (creator of Winnie the Pooh)

Give yourself time to organize your thoughts and plans before you implement them so you can take focused action and make the most of your "doing" time.

Step 2 - Set a time limit

Give yourself a set time frame to make your decision. Define it with a deadline or a timer. This puts a limit on research, exploration, and deliberation and emphasizes the actual decision itself.

Step 3 - Make the decision

The point of any decision is to enable action. When making decisions, your goal is simply to make the decision, not get hung up about making the *right* or *perfect* one.

In reality, you never get to see the whole picture before you make your first move.

"You don't have to see the whole staircase, just take the first step." —Martin Luther King Jr.

"Nothing will ever be attempted if all possible objections must be first removed."
—Samuel Johnson

Making the decision right in front of you is enough so you can run with it and take action. An imperfect decision that enables you to take action beats waiting on perfect conditions every time (see Way 21).

Try it with:

✓ Writing—the thought process of brainstorming, planning, and writing bullet points can be very different from the headspace for writing creatively and eloquently. Separate the task of deciding what to write about from the actual writing itself.

✓ Sales calls—Decide whom to call and what you are going to say first. Then tackle a batch of calls in a focused way, one after the other, to get them done (see Way 1).

✓ Any project—Set aside time to make the decisions of why (purpose), what (goal), how (actions), and when (timing), so that you have a plan to implement and can focus solely on taking action.

20

Manage Your Energy, Not Time

You can't really manage your time. We all have twenty-four hours in a day, and there is nothing you can do to make it last longer or go faster. But you *can* manage your energy.

Ever notice how you can get things done super quickly one day, and on another day it seems to drag and take forever? Chances are the difference was in your energy, not your time.

When you are "in the zone," fully charged and fired up, you think and move more quickly. You are more decisive and focused. You don't let distractions and doubt get in the way. If you are feeling low and lethargic, you are physically and mentally slower, and probably spend a lot more time sitting and staring at the computer screen.

Know your strengths

Strengths are the things that strengthen you. They're not just what you're good at, but they are what energize you.

Sometimes our strengths come so naturally, we take them for granted. Think about the last time you were really "in the flow" at work. What were you doing? What would you happily do all day, work hard at, and be buzzing from at the end of the day?

What are your strengths? Are you taking full advantage of them in your business?

Do the candle test

Draw a candle. Write all your business activities that energize you next to the flame. Put the ones that drain you by the wax.

How much of your time is spent "in the flame," and how much is "in the wax"? How does this affect your energy levels?

Tailor your time to your energy

When are your high-energy times during the day? When are you most alert? This is your prime time, so use it wisely. Schedule tasks that require you to be focused, fired up, and on the ball. Plan the more routine, mundane, or easier tasks for other times.

One of my clients found she was more creative in the mornings and better at implementation in the afternoon, so she scheduled her mornings for creation, ideas, and brainstorming, then switched into implementation mode to take these ideas to completion in the afternoon.

It's not just what you do, it's how you do it

You may not always be able to tailor your time exactly to your energy, so it's helpful to know how to boost your energy.

Does the thought of sitting in an office all day to work on your business plan bore you to death? Why not change how you do it? What would make it more inspiring, energetic, or fun?

Music, movement, and location can make a big difference. Get outdoors or change your working environment to be less—or more—structured. If you get your energy from being around people, make time to be with company. Or take space and time to be alone, if that's how you recharge.

Know what fuels you. Do you rise to a challenge and get competitive? Or are you more motivated by helping people and collaborating?

Know what energizes you and apply it to what you do and how you do it. The more appealing the task, the less energy you waste avoiding it, and the more enjoyment and satisfaction you get from accomplishing it.

Resources in this Way:

 Scan for more ways to boost your energy Grace-Marshall.com/ how-to-boost-energy-levels-in-the-evening

WAY 21

Choose Progress over Perfect

Perfectionism kills productivity in two ways: It stops us from getting started, because we want to get everything right before we start, and it stops us from finishing, when we keep doing and redoing, tweaking and editing before we actually consider it done.

Without getting it done, you don't see the value, and you don't see results. If you've got a ground-breaking revolutionary new product that never gets released, no ground gets broken and no-one's life gets revolutionized.

The blog you want to start or that novel you'd love to write? However thought provoking, inspiring, or genius, if it stays in draft form no one gets to read it. No one gets inspired and it makes absolutely zero impact.

The key to overcoming perfectionism is to realize that the value of anything is getting it done and out there. You make an impact when you release, publish, or deliver it—when you make it public.

Decide when good enough is good enough

Rather than aiming for flawlessness and spending all your time picking faults, be clear about what "job done" looks like. How good does it need to be? What key criteria must it fulfill? How will you know that your final outcome is good enough?

Set limits. Limit the number of retakes you allow yourself when you shoot a video. Limit the time you spend on editing. Set a completion date when you must publish, deliver, or ship your final project.

Take your learning forward

One of the biggest drivers behind perfectionism is the fear of making a mistake. Instead of beating yourself up with mistakes, take your learning forward. There will always be mistakes, improvements, and learning opportunities, and there are always things that you can do differently.

Rather than go back, rehash, re-edit, and go over the same things over and over again, take your learning forward, not backward.

Aim for progress

"The simple act of paying positive attention has a great deal to do with productivity." —Tom Peters

Perfection requires you to constantly fix, edit, and re-do what's imperfect. It requires you to focus on what's wrong. On the other hand, aiming for progress means you notice what's right and what's going well. The more attention you pay to progress, the more motivated you get to make *more* progress. The more you notice what's going well, the more you home in on what you're doing well, how you're doing it well, and how to leverage that to help you do more.

Focus on progress. Celebrate what you want to see more of. Write a "ta-da list" with your achievements each day and celebrate progress instead of perfect.

Conclusion

I hope this little book has inspired you with new ways to manage the stuff that sucks up your time. Play with them, experiment, adapt them, and make them yours. Enjoy making the most of your time and your talent!

About the Author

Grace Marshall is a life and business coach, NLP practitioner, DISC trainer and mom to two young children. She is passionate about helping busy business owners make the most of their time and their talents, and do life and business on their own terms.

She loves to encourage and equip entrepreneurs to design, create, and grow a business that works for them and their family, rather than the other way around—and still have time for the other important things in life, like friendship, fun, and rest!

Grace will be the first to admit she's not a naturally organized person. She doesn't believe there is such a thing as "perfect work/life balance" or in trying to "find more time." Instead, she's learned how to get stuff done in a way that works with her personality, lifestyle, and commitments. She now specializes in helping others tap into their unique strengths and natural working style with her personalized approach to productivity.

She lives in Stafford—somewhere in the middle of the U.K.—with her husband and their two children, where they are very much involved in a lively local church community. When she's not working (and sometimes when she is), you'll probably find her surrounded by people, books, music, or food—possibly even all at once.

To learn more about Grace, visit:
Grace-Marshall.com

Now that you know how to manage the stuff that sucks up your time, what would you *really* love to get done with your time?

Do you have a "someday" dream? One that you keep somewhere in the back of your mind as something you'd love to do someday?

Someday is a safe place to hide dreams. Safe from the scrutiny of whether it's doable, if you have what it takes and if it would work. Safe from the pressures of having to justify or validate your dream. Where everything is possible, but nothing ever gets done.

If you would like to take your dream out of "someday" and into reality, right here, right now. I invite you to download my 5 day email course "Dream to Done" to help you gain clarity, tackle barriers, overcome overwhelm, and take action to get your dream to done.

It's absolutely free, my gift to you.

Get it at Grace-Marshall.com/DreamToDone

Buckling from the weight of an ever-growing to-do list?

Fed up of trying to find more time?

If you want to:

- ✓ Get things done in the time that you have—no more trying to find time!
- ✓ Learn tools and techniques that work for you - even if you're not a "naturally organized" person
- ✓ Grow your business and make more money without sacrificing your family
- ✓ Enjoy guilt free time for what's important to you
- ✓ Start your day excited, fired up and ready to go and finish it with that feeling of deep satisfaction of a day well lived.

Then you'll love the Productivity Profits Guide

The busy person's guide to getting things done, so that you can enjoy more time for what's important to you and profit from your productivity.

Grace-Marshall.com/Productivity

"This is brilliant—I have found it to be absolutely invaluable and it has spurred me on to 'get my butt into gear' and get things moving in my business thanks to you and your Productivity Profits Guide.

Easy to listen to, easy to understand, highly motivational and well and truly stopped me procrastinating—I can't thank you enough!!!" —Sue Hatfield, "The Life Locksmith"

Collect them all!

21 WAYS to **write & publish** your non-fiction **book**
Kristen Eckstein

21 WAYS to **powerfully network** your business
Kristen Eckstein

21 WAYS to enjoy a **stress-free holiday** season
Dr. Daisy Sutherland

21 WAYS to make **money speaking**
Felicia J. Slattery, M.A., M.Ad.Ed.

21 WAYS to **skyrocket** your **creativity**
Tony Laidig

21 WAYS to be a **kid** again **& get adult results**
Kristen Eckstein

21 WAYS to **run** a stress-free **business**
Dr. Daisy Sutherland

21 WAYS to **manage** the **stuff** that **sucks up your time**
Grace Marshall

Look for more *21 Ways*™ books at
21WaysBooks.com

Lightning Source UK Ltd.
Milton Keynes UK
UKOW04f0921040716

277477UK00009B/17/P